Also by Jack Nicklaus
MY 55 WAYS TO LOWER YOUR GOLF SCORE

Take a Tip from Me

by

JACK NICKLAUS

WITH DRAWINGS BY FRANCIS GOLDEN

SIMON AND SCHUSTER
NEW YORK

LIBRARY OF CONGRESS CATALOG CARD NUMBER: 68-14843
MANUFACTURED IN THE UNITED STATES OF AMERICA

To Jack Grout,
my first and only teacher—
the man who taught me everything I know
about golf.

CONTENTS

Foreword   9
Some things to think about before you swing   15
Don't let your ego shorten your tee shots   16
The shot that is toughest of all   18
For a direct hit, tee the target high   20
Grip it like a club, not a rifle   23
A rule of thumb that strengthens your grip   25
Be sure you get the right slant   27
Cure for a stiff arm   28
Try your footwork to waltz time   30
There is no pause that refreshes   32
There are two sides to every tee   35
Not the time to be half safe   36
Getting the biggest bite from a dogleg   39
How to tell if everything is under control   40
What comes after dictates what comes first   43
Use your head—and use a tee   44
Hit short when preparing to play long   47
One way of getting back to business   48
A place that you must put the squeeze on   50
Use a helping hand to steady the head   53
Give the target the back of your hand   54
A place where gambling is proper   56
One way not to pull is to give the ball a push   59
You don't need a saw to handle a tree limb   60
A little "flaw" that is not a flaw   62
Your address changes with the loft of the club   64
If you are trapped by a tree, forget it   67
Exploding your way through grass   68

A trap shot that saves you strokes, but not in a trap   71
Bend your back when digging out of a ditch   73
Two to try when coming through the rye   75
It matters if you wiggle a toe   78
Try using half a swing for the half-pitch shot   81
Standing firm in the pines   82
Hitting fat? Go have your head examined   84
You can learn from a telltale divot mark   87
A woodsman's chop cuts through an impossible lie   88
An open approach for a treacherous sand   91
Hitting a one-hopper for the short stop   92
A small chip can beat a big blast   94
How you can survive an explosion   96
You don't need sand to use a sand wedge   98
A neglected shot to keep you out of trouble   101
Make your putter suit your game   102
An outrageous suggestion about putting   104
Know what your hands are up to   106
Where headwork means more than the swing   109
An overspin stroke smooths a bumpy route   110
An awful putt showed me how to win   113
"What's wrong with Nicklaus?"   115
Don't let your golf be a dirty business   119
Save strokes by being a divot digger   121
When a big club suits small boys   122
It isn't a game of inches   125

FOREWORD

Golf obviously is not a simple game, otherwise there would be no reason for me to convey the theories and principles that have been the basic framework for my game since I began to play golf as a ten-year-old at the Scioto Country Club in Columbus, Ohio. So permit me to caution you right now: Do not expect to take a tip from me and then march hastily to the first tee and promptly shoot the best round of your life. Golf demands practice and thought and proper execution, and the time it takes to read and study the tips in this book will not make you the club champion overnight. However, by applying what I say in this book, as well as reviewing my original instructional text, *My 55 Ways to Lower Your Golf Score,* you will, I am convinced, play consistently better golf, and that, after all, is what we all want to do.

Every golfer must, of course, have his teacher. My father, Charlie, who still plays a respectable game today, started me playing golf and taught me the interlocking grip I still use. Then he turned me over to Jack Grout, who then was the pro at Scioto and now is at LaGorce in Miami Beach. I can still remember taking group lessons with a dozen other ten-year-olds every Friday morning at Scioto. Jack attempted to change my grip from interlocking to the overlapping a few times, but after a week or so he always would tell me to hold the club my own way. I had and still have small hands, and the interlocking grip enables me to hold the club quite firmly.

There cannot be a nicer man anywhere than Jack Grout. He taught me everything I know about golf, except, of course, what I have learned from tournament competition. We worked on the fundamentals—grip, stance, hand and wrist actions, turns, weight shift, backswing, impact, follow through—everything. One important thing he taught me, too, was that it is not just how you play a golf shot a certain way but *why* you play it that way. After all, every golfer knows he must take the club away straight and hold his hands high at the top and bring the club down and through the ball. But does he know *why*? When you can answer the question *why,* then you know your golf swing, and consequently when a flaw develops in your swing you can make your own correction. All because you know *why*. Bobby Jones told me once the reason he slumped for several years was that he did not know his own swing. And he said he did not consider himself a great golfer until he learned the swing.

I also was quite fortunate during my early golfing years because my father never insisted that I play golf or, for that matter, any other sport. He introduced me to every sport there was—football, basketball, baseball, tennis (I still play for exercise), golf—everything. I selected the ones I liked best and concentrated on them.

My father won eleven letters in high school, and he played three sports in college and also won the Columbus City Tennis Championship one year. He loved sports. I know it broke his heart when I gave up football in high school to play in my first National Amateur. Never, though, did he attempt to persuade me to play any sport. I intend to follow his example with my own boys, Jackie, six, and Stevie, four. I will not put a driver in their hands and make them hit hundreds of golf balls every day. They will play whatever sports they prefer.

Playing competitive golf most of the year, in twenty to twenty-five tournaments throughout the United States, in ten or twelve exhibitions, in matches over in England and down in Australia, also requires an understanding wife. I, thankfully, have one. Barbara knows what my business is, and she realizes what sacrifices we both must make for me to play in a tournament in, say, Palm Springs or Pittsburgh.

This book is a compendium of the instructional tips and feature-length stories that appear under my by-line in *Sports Illustrated*. The tips started as a ten-part series shortly after I turned professional and joined the tour in 1962, and now they appear in approximately twenty-five issues a year. I spend many hours with the magazine's editorial consultant working over a tape recorder and then later posing for the highly technical pictures that are used for the drawings illustrating each tip. I study and approve both art work and narrative before the tip appears in print.

The tips probably can be classified in three categories: 1) technical explanations of how to better your swing, 2) strategical explanations of how to prepare yourself mentally for your round of golf, and 3) practical explanations of how to play situation shots. Generally the ideas for these tips result from actual experience during a tournament. For instance, included in this book is a tip about playing a shot from a trap that has sand quite like bits of glass, and playing from it presents new problems, as I discovered. And I tell you how to play a shot to the green even though a tree limb is staring at you. For strategy, there is a tip telling you when to gamble with your shots, and another telling you how to prepare for a tournament or just a friendly round at a course considerably longer or shorter than your own club's. And for the technical aspects about the theory of the swing, we talk about your thumb and your wrists, your knees and your hips, your shoulder and your head. Also included in this book are two long stories I wrote for *Sports Illustrated*. The first tells how I discovered a major flaw in my putting by watching the video tape of the final round of the 1966 Masters and then won a play-off the next day thanks to good putting. The second reveals how I won the U.S. Open in 1967: I changed my game back to a left-to-right fade, found a new white-headed putter and started to "pop" my putts again.

The techniques and explanations described in this book are my own, and although they may not conform to what you have read elsewhere, they have been quite beneficial to me. I hope they will be as beneficial to you.

—JACK NICKLAUS

Take
a Tip
from Me

JACK NICKLAUS

Some things to think about
before you swing

In golf as in, say, alligator wrestling, the approach to the problem can be everything. Here are two planning thoughts that seem basic, yet most golfers ignore them. The first is the matter of really being certain how far away the green is. I am known for my habit of pacing off a course during practice rounds and making notes on a scorecard of how far a certain rock or tree is from a green. From then on, when my ball is anywhere in the area of one of my measuring points I know the exact distance to the pin. The guesswork is gone. I don't care how deceptive the distance may look, because I will not judge the distance by eye. I let my notes tell me how hard to hit the approach shot. Have you ever made such notes for your own course? Most likely you have not. Try it, and you will be surprised at how easy correct club selection becomes.

Second, always plan your game to suit the course that you are playing. Take, for example, the Firestone course in Akron, Ohio, and Whitemarsh in Philadelphia. There is not one easy birdie hole at Firestone. There is no place that you can gamble and still make a par if you fail. If you come up with a 6 or 7, you cannot regain the strokes with birdies. So you should not gamble. At Whitemarsh, however, there are four relatively short par-5 holes where prospects for birdies are excellent. With this in mind, you should play a bolder game and gamble for birdies on every hole at Whitemarsh. In short, make your plan of attack suit the course.

An annotated scorecard ends club-selection guesswork, and preround strategy saves you strokes on the course.

Don't let your ego
shorten your tee shots

Many golfers make the mistake of thinking that a high-compression ball—that is, one wound very tightly—will automatically give the most distance. But more often than not, the reverse is true. To get maximum distance you must use a ball with a resiliency that matches the speed of your swing. The slower the swing, the softer the ball should be, because the more your club head flattens the ball at impact, up to a certain point, the farther it will go. If your swing is an easy one and the ball is too hard, it will feel and react like a rock. However, if your swing is hard and your ball is too soft, you will not get maximum results either. All manufacturers rate their golf balls according to compression. The softer the ball, the lower compression rating it has. Because they generate so much club-head speed, the long-hitting pros use a high-compression ball, one rated between 95 and 100. This ball will compress just enough to give them maximum distance. Most other pros use balls rated between 90 and 95. These compression ratios are too high for the average golfer. Even most low-handicap players should stick with a compression ratio between 75 and 90. Soft swingers and high handicappers will achieve maximum distance with a ball in the 60-to-75 compression range. Consult your pro to find the right compression ball for you. It may be hard on your self-esteem, but use the ball best suited to your swing.

When the weekend golfer hits a softer ball he gets proper compression and thus more distance than with the hard ball.

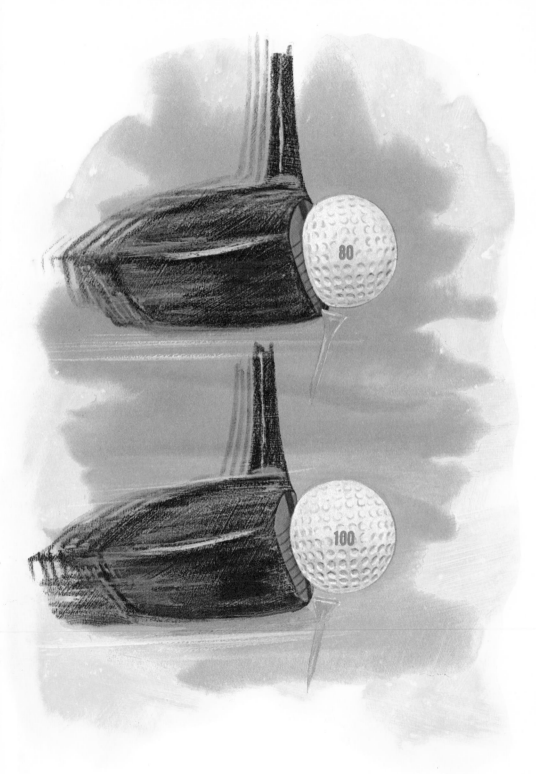

17

You are on the first tee. You are not really warmed up, have not played for a week, have plenty of spectators and want to go hide.

The shot that is

toughest of all

What is the hardest shot in golf? You will get votes for the wedge off dirt or the 100-yard explosion or the any-old-thing out of a clover patch. But why overlook the one shot which, unless you are most unusual, rattles you every time you try it, yet you have to try it every time you play? I mean, of course, the drive off the first tee. It is like the opening of a football game. I am nervous until the action starts, and I imagine you have the same feeling. What happens next is that most of us try to hurry because we want to get it over with. We are too keyed up to hit a decent shot, but we swing anyway, just as fast as we

can. The result is often a disastrous start for what becomes a bad round.

What I try to do is to pretend that I am relaxed. I take a few deep breaths and swing my driver lazily back and forth to encourage a mood of composure. Next, I try very hard to think of nothing but hitting the ball. I don't think about myself or what is at stake or what the people watching might think about my swing. I just concentrate on meeting the ball as solidly as I can. Finally, I slow down my swing. I take the club back more slowly than usual, and I make the down-swing as unforced as possible. The result often is the best drive of the day just when it is wanted the most.

For a direct hit, tee the target high

How high you should tee a ball is another of those seemingly insignificant elements of golf that can matter a great deal. There is no point in working out something as complex as the pivot if you then ruin shots by being careless about the simple things. The basic rule is that the ball should be teed at the same height every time. Do not ever let the contour of the fairway dictate how high you tee up. Some players tee the ball low if the fairway slopes downhill and high if it rises in front of the tee. This is an error that leads to inconsistent shots. When playing into the wind, of course, you should tee the ball low and hit it low, or you will lose too much distance. On almost all other occasions, however, the ball should be high enough so that when the club head rests on the ground about half the ball shows above it. Ideally, you are going to swing just a little above the top of the grass. As the drawing at the right shows, you will thus hit the ball in the center of the club face.

This ball may seem to be teed too high, for when the driver is in the address position half of the ball shows above the club head. But if the swing is correct the club will be slightly above the grass at impact and will meet the ball solidly.

Greater club control is achieved when the right forefinger is pressed firmly against the middle finger (arrow).

The hands tend to work against one another if the trigger finger is stretched away from the middle finger.

Grip it like a club, not a rifle

In most discussions of the golf grip excessive attention is paid to how many knuckles should be visible or which eyeball the Vs should point at, and too little to how the fingers should actually be placed on the shaft. Take the so-called trigger finger of the right hand, for instance. Many players, more through carelessness than by design, put their right hand on the club as if they were actually pulling a trigger. In other words, the trigger finger is stretched away from the middle finger (*left*). To my way of thinking, this is a mistake. A good grip has the hands working together; they are not two separate entities fighting for control of the club. The more space the hands take up, the more difficult it will be for them to work together. The less space, the more control they will be able to exercise. So resist the temptation to reach for a trigger the next time you grip a club. Keep all of your fingers snugly together.

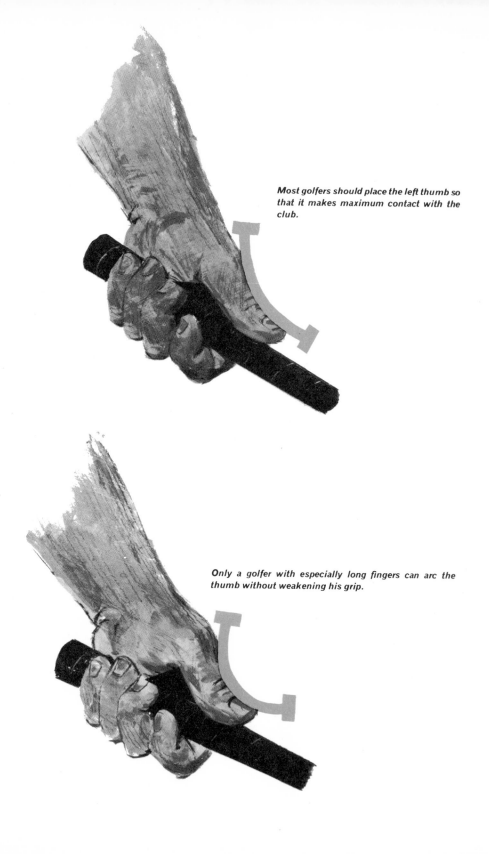

Most golfers should place the left thumb so that it makes maximum contact with the club.

Only a golfer with especially long fingers can arc the thumb without weakening his grip.

A rule of thumb

that strengthens your grip

How the left thumb should be placed on top of the shaft does not seem a likely subject of controversy, but golf pros—teachers and tournament players alike—have varying views on the matter. Should the thumb be pressed down firmly? Should it be loose? Should it lie full length along the top of the shaft? If you want a good, solid grip the answer to those questions is surprisingly important. The weekend golfer tends simply to grasp the club with the left hand, wrap the right hand over it and call it a day. This is regrettable, because the thumb can be one of the anchors of a good grip. My feeling is that the more thumb touching the shaft, the more solid the grip is likely to be. This is especially true in the case of golfers like myself, who have relatively small hands and need all the actual contact with the club that they can get. So I push my left thumb as far down the shaft as it will comfortably go, and thus obtain additional control of the club and a little extra feel, which I need. There is one exception to this rule. A player with very long fingers already has sufficient hand control. If he stretches the thumb down the shaft he may interfere with the grip of the right hand. But the rest of us should not just let that left thumb sit there like a useless hunk of putty. So stretch it out and use it.

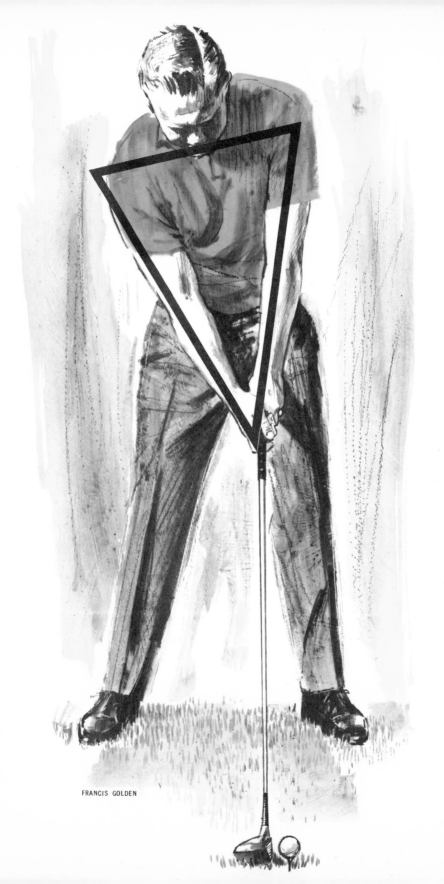

FRANCIS GOLDEN

Be sure you get the right slant

The position of the shoulders at address is one of the least involved but most important aspects of golf. Properly positioned, the shoulders can be the key to a very good swing. Improperly set, they start a chain reaction of wrong moves. For example, if your shoulders are level at address—parallel to the ground—then your hands have to start off well behind the ball. As a result, you may find that during the swing you are making some unnatural adjustment to get your hands forward and into the correct hitting position. However, if your shoulders are properly angled, your hands almost have to get into their correct position during the swing.

To set your shoulders, first place your feet, then hold your club and stand up straight. Next, relax your shoulders slightly, and as you take your normal grip and place the club behind the ball notice how your right shoulder drops until it is somewhat lower than the left. This is the correct position. Do not exaggerate it by dropping the right shoulder more or forcing the left shoulder up.

The shoulders and arms should form a tilted triangle, with the right shoulder well below the left, as the backswing is about to begin.

Before gripping the club, relax the shoulders so that the arms hang limply at each side.

Cure for a stiff arm

The well-executed golf swing is an athletic movement so filled with unnatural twists and turns that any chance to make it more natural should be eagerly seized upon. The position of the elbows at address offers a perfect illustration of what I mean. I know that some golfers think the elbows should be pressed toward each other as if wrapped in a giant rubber band, and that others vigorously twist their arms so that the elbow points are aimed at their belt buckle and their arm muscles are coiled like chunks of rope. This kind of rigidity may be all right

At address your arms remain relaxed, with the flat inside of each elbow turned inward.

for a man who knows exactly what he is doing. In fact, Gary Player always sets himself up this way. But most players attempting this will end up with too much tension, a stiff swing and a poor shot. What I try to do is keep my arms supple at address, let them feel natural. You can do this, too, if you will go through a regular routine until it becomes habit. Start by relaxing your shoulders so that they even droop somewhat. Then drop your arms to your sides so that they hang in a natural position. Finally, simply reach out and take your grip on the club. Your elbows will then remain in the same relative position they were in while hanging loosely at your sides, and your arms will be free of unnecessary, unwanted tension.

Try your footwork to waltz time

Learning the footwork for a golf swing is a little like learning the waltz. You are attempting to develop tempo and rhythm, and the best way to do it is to go off somewhere by yourself and give it a try: one-two-three, one-two-three. Begin by taking a narrower stance than normal, for this allows you to exaggerate the rocking motion of the feet. Now try a chip-shot swing—with or without a club—and feel how the feet move. Then extend the swing by degrees as you get

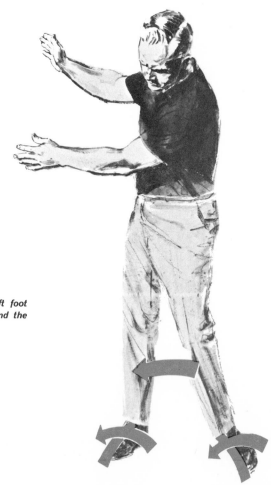

In a simulated backswing, the left foot rocks fairly sharply on its side, and the hands establish tempo.

loosened up, until you eventually are using the body action required for a tee shot. The left foot should be rolling in on the backswing, and the right foot rolling in on the downswing. As your swing gets longer your heels are going to come off the ground slightly, the left heel on the backswing and the right heel on the follow-through, but this should be kept to a minimum. Ideally, it would be better—without disrupting the rest of your swing—if you could keep the left heel on the ground all the time, but I can't. My own left heel lifts when I extend my swing to the four or five iron. In addition to helping your footwork, this exercise will also improve your hand action.

In the follow-through of the footwork exercise, the weight shifts to the left foot, and the right heel lifts slightly.

There is no pause that refreshes

You often hear golfers talk about "the pause at the top of the back-swing," but this is a very misleading phrase. If you start thinking that there is literally a pause at the top of your swing—and try to make sure that you do pause—you are going to ruin your game, for there is no single point in the backswing where everything comes to a grand halt, as if you were posing for a photograph. The reason is that the

This is the end of the backswing, with the body turned and the weight on the right side.

instant your hips have moved as far back as they should, they must immediately start forward. The two illustrations below show clearly what happens. At the left I have reached the end of my backswing, my weight is on my right side and my hips have turned well to the right. Note the angle of the club to the ground. In the drawing at right I have started the downswing. My weight has shifted and my hips are turning forward but, as you can see, the club has not yet moved. The club has stopped—paused, if you will—because my arms must wait for my body turn to generate power, but in no sense has there been a pause in the swing as a whole. If you do literally stop your swing, you usually will end up taking a powerless swipe at the ball with just your arms.

The forward action starts at once, even though the club remains in the same position.

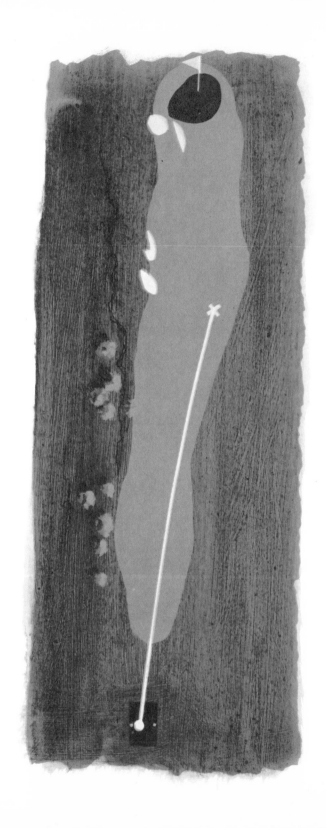

There are two sides to every tee

Golf is a game in which you must seize every advantage you can get. By paying attention to a lot of seemingly inconsequential things you may make a very consequential difference in your score. Consider the simple matter of where you should place the ball on the tee. It may appear unimportant, but it isn't. The first thing to find, of course, is a good flat spot. On a reasonably well-kept course the tee will be uniformly flat, so you have a choice as to which side of the tee to use. The decision is an easy one, but few golfers know how to make it. If there is trouble on the left side of the fairway, you should hit from the left side of the tee. This enables you to aim toward the right side of the fairway and away from the trouble. If there are hazards on the right, tee up on the right. When there is a crosswind, it, too, becomes a factor. When the wind is left to right, tee up on the left side and try to fade the ball slightly with the wind, thus getting as much yardage as possible out of your shot. If the wind is right to left, use the right side of the tee and attempt to pull the shot a little, again giving the wind a maximum chance to carry the ball while still keeping it on the fairway.

If trees and traps line the left side of the fairway, hit the ball from the left of the tee while aiming the shot away from the trouble.

Not the time to be half safe

The golf hole at the right illustrates the concepts involved in tee-shot management. There are four bunkers surrounding the area in which you would like to hit your drive. Even though the safe section of the fairway is only 15 or 20 yards wide at any point, you say to yourself, "I'll have an easy second shot to the green with a six iron if I can hit the driver between the bunkers." You don't stop to think what happens if you miss your target area—the odds of hitting it are against you—and land in a bunker. This is a case where you should use an iron off the tee and land short of the bunkers, planning then to hit a longer iron to the green. There is an ample target area short of the bunkers, and it should not be difficult for you to get a two- or three-iron shot into a safe position. This is a tactic that all of us used repeatedly during the 1966 British Open at Muirfield, and I must say that in my case, at least, the results were most rewarding.

When the ideal landing area (striped section) is tightly bunkered, an iron off the tee may be the perfect answer.

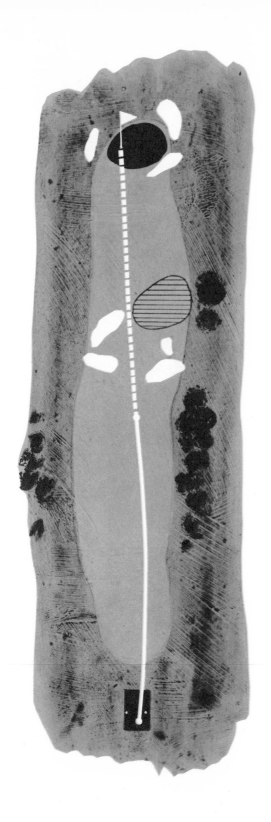

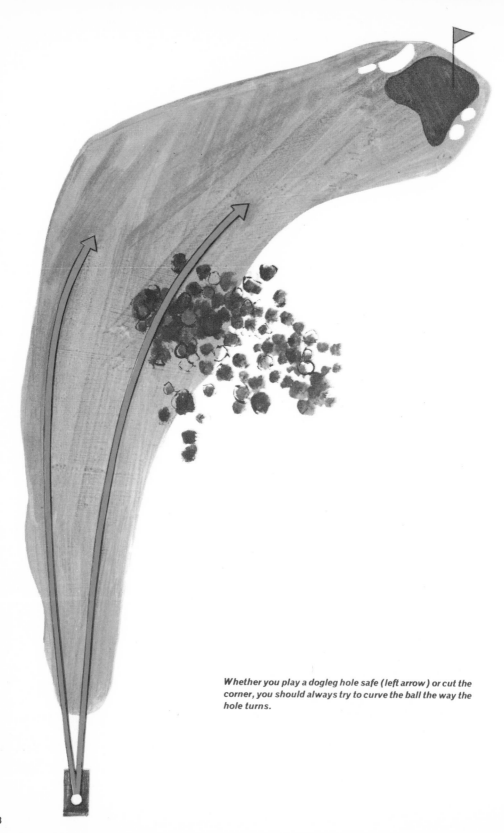

Whether you play a dogleg hole safe (left arrow) or cut the corner, you should always try to curve the ball the way the hole turns.

Getting the

biggest bite from a dogleg

The pleasure of playing a dogleg hole lies in the opportunity it presents off the tee. Depending on your courage and your ability with a drive, the hole can often be made to play just as short or as long as you want it to. The primary thing to consider about a dogleg hole, of course, is the possibility of cutting across the corner and setting up an easy shot to the green. If the penalty for failing to carry the corner is not too severe, you should very likely try it. But be smart about it. Always attempt to play the shot to follow the contour of the hole. Let us say the hole bends from left to right and the trouble is in the bend, where it usually is on a dogleg. If you are not going to cut the corner, aim your tee shot at the left side of the fairway and try to fade it toward the center of the fairway. This will let you get maximum roll and give you the best chance of ending up as close as possible to the green without taking the totally unnecessary risk of hitting the tee shot right at the corner of the dogleg. If you decide to cut the corner, you should still try to bend the shot in the direction of the dogleg. It takes a little nerve, but if failure won't ruin you, cross over the corner with a fade on a hole that doglegs from left to right and hit a hook over the bend on a hole that goes from right to left. You say you can't hit an intentional hook or slice? Perhaps you naturally hook or slice. If you do, cut the corners that go the way you usually curve the ball, and never try to cut a corner that goes the other way.

How to tell if
everything is under control

Many golfers think that overswinging automatically creates more power, that there is a direct ratio between the size of the swing and the power it generates. But this thinking is wrong. You get maximum power only by swinging within what I like to think of as the confines of your feet. There are two basic rules governing this: (1) you do not want to let your weight be on the outside of your right foot during the backswing, and (2) you do not want your weight on the outside of your left foot until after you make contact with the ball. Here is how I work with the knees, ankles and feet during my swing. I start with my weight evenly distributed on the balls of my feet. As I shift my weight to the inside of my right foot on the backswing, I roll my left foot in. The left knee turns in naturally, but the right knee remains fairly stationary. Now, as I come into the ball, my right knee turns and my weight moves off the ball of my right foot and onto my left. The right knee, meanwhile, is moving straight at the hole. After impact the weight moves farther, until it is on the outside of the left foot. Eventually my weight is far to the left, and my right heel is well off the ground. This may give the impression of overswinging, but it is not until the ball has been hit that the weight gets outside of the left foot.

The right knee has hardly moved at the completion of the backswing (left), but is flying forward after impact.

What comes after

dictates what comes first

It is obvious that you can hit a good shot even if you follow through awkwardly, for nothing you do after the ball leaves the club head is going to influence where the ball goes. But a sound follow-through is still a vital element in a golf swing because it helps insure that everything that went before was done properly. What is a good follow-through? In general, there are three important elements to look for: (1) how the hands finish, (2) how the right shoulder finishes and (3) the position of the head.

Ideally, the hands should finish high. This indicates that you have brought them straight through the impact area and out toward the target. If the hands finish past and below the left shoulder, it usually means the swing has been too flat or the wrists have rolled over excessively at impact. At the same time, the right shoulder should stay down and underneath the left. This indicates that you have hit straight through the ball with all your power, and not pulled the face of the club across it. Finally, the head should be kept down but slightly tilted, to the point where you watch the flight of the ball almost entirely out of the corner of your left eye. This means you have maintained a steady position throughout the swing and stayed down on the shot.

In a perfect follow-through the hands finish high, the right shoulder is kept down and below the left shoulder, and the head is pointed down, with the golfer barely able to see to the left.

Use your head—and use a tee

When you can have a perfect lie, why give yourself a mediocre one? This is a question I ask on the frequent occasions when I see golfers, both good ones and bad, hitting a tee shot on a par-3 hole without teeing up the ball. These players simply drop the ball on the ground and roll it around with the club head until they get what they think is a satisfactory lie. But there is a chance that the lie is not satisfactory, and it certainly is not the best lie possible. On even the most closely mowed tees, blades of grass will come between the club face and the

ball if the ball is not clear of the ground. The grass reduces the backspin that the club can put on the ball, and also accents the effect of any mistakes in the swing. The most frequent result is a shot that holds its line fairly well but "sails," ending up over the green. A par-3 hole can be hard enough without making it tougher through carelessness. What you should do is tee the ball up so that it sits above the top of the grass. The club is then free to make clean, crisp contact with the ball.

When the ball is teed up (opposite left) the club head can get at it cleanly and the club-face grooves can impart maximum backspin. But if the ball is simply put on the ground (below), grass can get between the club head and the ball and affect the shot.

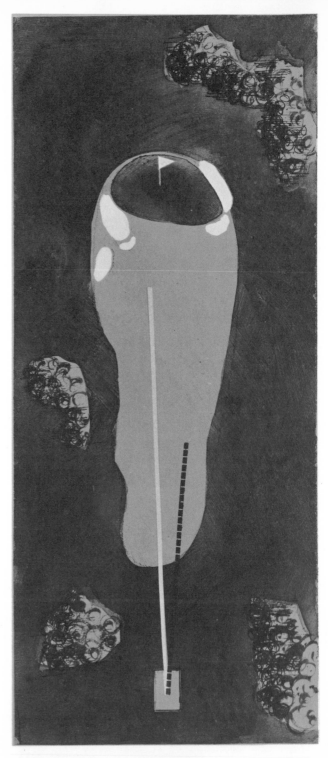

Deliberately hitting a short tee shot (dotted line) instead of using a driver (solid line) will help get your game ready for a long course.

Hit short when

preparing to play long

Getting yourself ready to play a golf course that is considerably longer or shorter than your usual one presents certain problems in shot adjustment. For instance, if you normally use a driver and short irons on your own 6,400-yard course, you cannot expect to hit drivers and long irons on a 6,900-yard course and score well without preparation. Quite often when I am preparing to play a tournament at an extremely long course, I will go out with an 8 to 10 handicapper at home in Columbus and hit *his* second shots, which means that I am forced to play a lot of long irons, many of them from difficult angles into the green. (One time at Scioto, in Columbus, I played the tee shots of a friend who got his drives into the fairway only three times. This wasn't much practice for me, but I shot one of the best 79s of my life.) If you are getting ready for a course much longer than your own, you too should adjust your game. Instead of hitting a drive and wedge on the 340-yard hole, hit a five iron off the tee and then another long iron to the green. The primary reason for this is not to give you practice swinging a long iron. You can get that on a practice tee. The purpose is to become accustomed to hitting into the green from a considerable distance so that the long course you are headed for does not mentally defeat you before you start.

One way of getting back to business

Golf is a friendly, sociable game, and it should be played that way. Unfortunately, however, it is not always easy to be sociable and still maintain the concentration that you must have to play your best. Some people who watch me in tournaments get the idea that I am too single-minded and taciturn to get any fun out of golf. This is not so. I am actually pretty talkative on the course, and I enjoy the company of my fellow competitors as much as anyone on the tour. But I have had to work out a way of being able to be friendly and still gather my full concentration when I am about to hit a shot. Since this is a problem that is common to all golfers, my solution might work well for you, too.

As you get set over the ball, assemble your concentration by thinking of one specific thing; in this case, looking at the divot mark after the shot is hit.

As you first walk up to the ball, think what kind of shot would be perfect for the occasion—high, low, hook, fade, etc. This will snap your mind back to the job at hand. Second, as you get set to hit the shot, try to concentrate on just one thing that you want to do during the swing. It might be "keep your head down," or "look at the divot after you've hit," or "make a full shoulder turn." Thinking of something specific will insure that your mind is not wandering at the moment it must be attending to business.

A place that you must put the squeeze on

Squeeze grip firmly just before starting backswing, then draw club back slowly.

If you frequently have days when your swing seems right but the shots still go all wrong, you may be doing what the pros call "losing the club" at the top of the swing. This is one of golf's most common errors. What it amounts to, basically, is that the fingers of the left hand have lost their hold on the club just as it reaches the final stages of the backswing. This permits the club to flop around like a wet towel. The resulting shot goes almost anywhere—but seldom where it is aimed. The main cause of this error is an excessively fast backswing. The club is yanked away from the ball so quickly that the fingers do not have enough strength to maintain control at the top. But there are other possible causes, too, so various cures must be tried. Begin by

Grip must remain tight at top, and will if swing is smooth and wrists cock late.

keeping your hands loose on the club until just before starting the backswing. Do not tighten them until the last possible second. I substitute this squeezing of the club for the last-moment forward press that is used by so many professionals. The tightening action serves as a sort of trigger to start the backswing. Next, do not jerk the club away from the ball as you start it back. Instead, concentrate on maintaining a smooth, unhurried tempo. Tempo is everything. Finally, do not consciously cock the wrists during the backswing. The natural force of the backswing will make the wrists cock in their own good time, so forget them. Follow these three steps and your grip should be as firm at the top of the backswing as it was at the start.

Use a helping hand

to steady the head

So many good shots are hit by the golfer who can keep his head steady throughout the swing and so many bad ones by the golfer who cannot that mastering this fundamental is obviously worth all the effort involved. A golfer whose head sways will lose not only power but direction. If his head sways back or dips he is likely to hit behind the ball. If his head sways toward the target the chances are he will hit one of golf's most annoying and expensive shots, the cold top, which leaves a scowl on the face of the golfer and a smile on the now useless ball. I have a practice technique that may help you if you have tried less drastic remedies and are still having trouble keeping your head steady. While you hit practice shots with a short iron, have a friend lean toward you with his hand placed firmly on the top of your head (*left*) to hold it in a steady position. Hit as many shots as your friend is willing to stand still for, all the while swinging smoothly through the ball as you try to get the feel of the proper rotation. If this does not seem to help, you can go one step further. Have your obliging assistant grab a handful of hair and tell him to hang on tight. Now you will know immediately and memorably if your head moves even a fraction of an inch while you swing.

By practicing under the pressure of a firm hand, you learn to rotate your shoulders around an immovable head as if you were a well-oiled piece of machinery.

Give the target
the back of your hand

Whether you have a gun in your hand or a golf club, if you expect to hit a target you must first take aim. Because so many parts of the body—hands, feet, knees, hips and shoulders—are involved, taking aim in golf is a complicated process. Let's consider just the matter of the hands. Do you have the habit of taking your grip on the club while you are waving it around in the air? Many golfers do, but this is a very inaccurate way of getting the club face and the hands on line. You should begin by placing the club head on the ground behind the ball and squaring the face to the target. Then, keeping the club firmly in place, position your left hand so that the back of the hand is also aimed directly at the target. Next, place the right hand on the club so that its palm is square to the same line. Now your hands and the club face are properly aligned, and at least one error has been eliminated right at the very beginning. This step-by-step method of taking the grip makes adjusting for a draw or a fade relatively easy. For a right-to-left draw you merely turn the club face slightly to the left of the line to the target; for a left-to-right fade, turn the club face slightly to the right of this line.

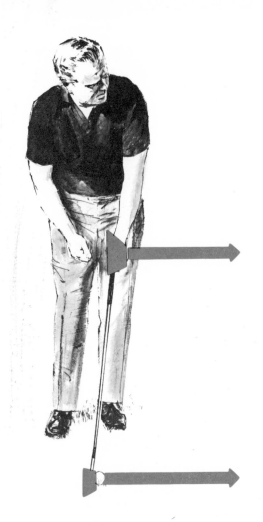

In taking your grip, hold the club so that both the club face and the left hand are aimed along the target line.

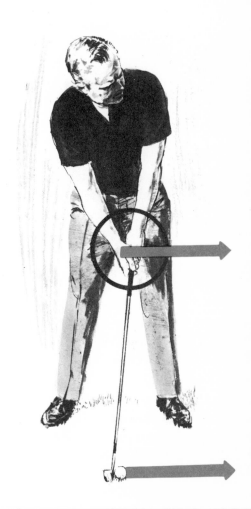

Now place the right hand on the club so that the palm is square to the line along which you are aiming.

A place where gambling is proper

Too often the weekend amateur does not give himself his best chance to reach the long par 4s or even the par 5s in two shots. He is prudent with his drive, and this frequently means that he has to play his second shot safely short of hazards guarding the front of the green. My advice on such holes, especially if there is any room at all off the tee, is to abandon caution. Stand up on the tee and decide to hit your longest possible drive, for this is a case in which boldness is not only much more fun, it is smart golf. As far as the touring pros are concerned, the 15th hole at the Augusta National, a par 5 with the same characteristics as the one at right, provides a good example of how this strategy works. We all try to hit big drives here because the reward for good tee shots can be great, while the penalty for bad ones is very slight. If, in our effort to swing hard, we hit sloppy drives we can still play safely short of the water with our second shots. Thus we are no worse off than the cautious player who has simply tried to steer his drive down the middle. The average golfer faces the same kind of challenge on his club's long par 4s. If he really cuts loose off the tee he opens up the chance to get home in two and possibly score a birdie. If his tee shot is poor he can usually hit a recovery shot out in front of the green, which is where he would have been anyway if he had hit a short, safe drive.

The advantage of boldness on a long par 4 or short par 5 is apparent here. With a big drive (solid black line) the green can be reached in two. If the drive is missed (solid red line, right) you can still be as well off as with two conservative shots (dotted red line, left).

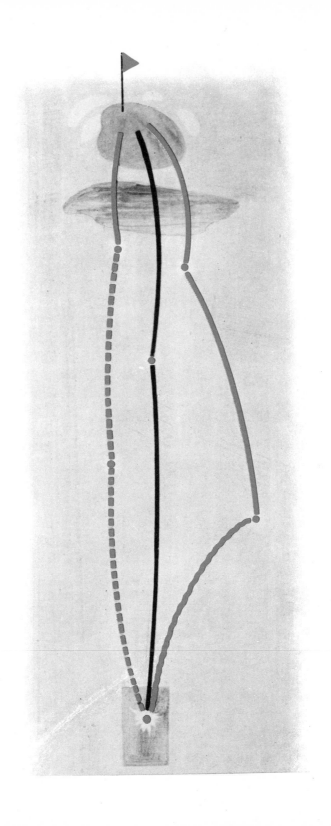

One way not to pull

is to give the ball a push

A pulled iron shot is a nuisance, in part because when you pull one you tend to repeat the mistake, much as you do when you start shanking. The pull, of course, does not look too bad; it does not hook or slice and feels firm coming off the club head, but it ends up 20 to 30 yards to the left of the green. There are three common causes for pulling an iron: 1) hitting the ball with an outside-in swing, 2) closing the club face somewhere during the swing and 3) starting with the ball too far forward in the stance. The first thing to do is check your stance. Every iron shot should be hit off the left heel, but no farther forward than that. Now concentrate on taking the club head back in a straight line and bringing it into the ball on the same straight line. Finally, make sure that the follow-through throws the club head out toward the hole and that you finish with your hands high, for a proper follow-through makes it almost impossible to pull the ball. If you feel that the rhythm of your swing is sound and that you are making good contact with the ball, you may succeed with the simplest cure of all for a pulled shot: try to push the shot instead. By concentrating on pushing the ball you may well move the club head into the proper groove.

The pulled iron (dotted line) can be prevented by concentrating on hitting through to the hole.

The predicament illustrated here is not uncommon. You are about 100 yards from the green but a low-hanging tree branch some 10 to 20 yards in front of you is keeping you from hitting a normal nine-iron approach. What is required is a shot that will carry no farther than a nine iron, but start off with the trajectory of a seven iron. Either club can be used—the seven iron by choking down on the grip and then hitting the ball almost normally, or the nine iron. I much prefer the latter, but certain swing adjustments are necessary. You must shut the face of the club, move the ball back toward the middle

of the stance and keep the hands well ahead of the ball. This has the effect of reducing the loft of the iron. Finally, place all the weight on the left side and leave it there throughout the swing. The result will be a firm nine-iron shot that has the normal amount of bite, but one that takes off low and gets under the tree limb.

When an approach shot must be kept low (left) the hands are moved ahead of the ball (right) and the weight is on the left side.

MY WAY: The right elbow moves slightly away from my body, but it still points down, and the club points toward the hole.

A so-called fundamental precept of golf that I do not hold with—at least, not all the way—maintains that if you don't keep the right elbow folded in against the body you cannot develop a grooved swing. No one has to look very closely at my swing to note that I let my own elbow stick out somewhat. Some critics have described this as a flaw in my swing, but I allow it to happen for what I consider to be two very good reasons. First, it permits me to take a more upright swing, one that actually makes it easier for me to keep the club head square and on line to the target. Second, it gives my swing a longer arc and thus enables me to get more power into my shots than I ordinarily would be able to.

Letting my elbow "fly" out certainly does not mean that my swing is not grooved or that it is likely to get out of control. In fact, my right elbow does not really fly. Throughout most of the backswing it is pointed in the general direction of the ground, and on the downswing it returns to the more traditional position, close to the body. By doing this, I feel I am getting all of the advantage of keeping the right elbow in close, without losing power. If your own swing is basically sound and you would like to try for a little more distance, see what happens when you move your right elbow away from your body.

INCORRECT: This is the real "flying elbow." The forearm is parallel to the ground, and the club points too far to the right.

Your address changes

with the loft of the club

Golf becomes easier whenever you can eliminate any variable that pertains to the swing, yet the classic methods of teaching involved some complex changes in ball positioning. The traditional theory for hitting irons stated that as the loft of the club increased, the position of the ball at address shifted to the right and the stance became more and more open. Every club, therefore, required its own stance. The system I use—as do most of today's touring pros—is much simpler. The right foot is moved closer to the left as the loft of the club increases, and the ball is positioned slightly closer to the golfer, because the shaft of the club is shorter. But regardless of the club being used, the stance always is kept square to the line of flight and the ball is always played off the left heel.

Whether the shot is a short iron or a long one, the ball should be played off the left heel.

If you are trapped by a tree, forget it

The best way to approach the situation illustrated here might be to put yourself into a trance. Every golfer tends to miss a high percentage of shots out of serious trouble, such as this one in which a tree limb is restricting the backswing, and all too often the reason for the miss is not the awkward lie but a failure to concentrate on execution. You begin to think about the tree instead of about hitting the ball. What you should do for any such shot is to take your position over the ball and try a tentative backswing. Once you have established how far back you can take the club, repeat the restricted swing over and over again—sometimes hitting the obstacle—until you are accustomed to swinging within the confines of the space available. Once you have done this, forget about the obstacle and put all of your concentration into the act of striking the ball firmly and properly. Even if you find that the club hits the tree on the backswing, you are now prepared for this and your unusual concentration will enable you to complete the shot.

Before trying a shot on which your swing is restricted, repeatedly test how far back you can take the club.

through grass

The swing is that of the normal bunker shot, with an outside-in arc (left), weight to the left and strong follow-through (right).

Here is a peculiar shot that comes up much more often than you might think, not only on courses in sandy area but around bunkers everywhere. I faced it twice in the Doral Open this spring, and both times I played it less than perfectly before learning why. The ball is in grass, or has tufts of grass around it, but the surrounding material is mostly loose sand. I always thought there were two alternatives with such a shot: play a delicate chip, picking the ball clean, or hit a regular bunker-type explosion. But I found—in spite of the fact that it demands more nerve—that the shot *must* be played as an explosion. The sand provides a cushion, more of one than you think will be there when you inspect the lie. By coming into the ball firmly with a sand wedge and using a strong right hand, you can get the shot up quickly and with lots of backspin. The heavy blade of the wedge will tear right through the tufts of grass as if they were not there.

A trap shot

that saves you strokes,

but not in a trap

Here is a "trap" shot that is not played from sand, but can help you when conditions are hazardous. Used frequently on seaside courses when the wind is high and a lot of roll is desired, the shot gets its name from the way the ball is trapped between the club head and the ground at impact. It is a favorite shot among certain pros—Arnold Palmer, Deane Beman and Gardner Dickinson use it often—and the weekend golfer should consider it, for it is not overly difficult. The ball is played well back in the stance, but the hands are kept in their normal position —which means they are now considerably ahead of the ball. The club face is shut at address, and the club head is taken straight back in order to avoid shutting the face too much during the swing. The downswing is controlled by the *right* hand, and the ball is hit down upon, almost as if you were trying to drive it into the ground. After contact, however, the follow-through is natural. The ball will take off straight, remain low and roll forever instead of rising to a peak and dropping softly. Because of the extra roll you should use one or two clubs less than you would normally.

Instead of being off the left heel (arrow), the ball is far back, the club head is started back straight and the right hand controls the swing.

Bend your back

when digging out of a ditch

Swinging at a golf ball that is well below the level of your stance, say in a gully or a ditch, should be a backbreaking business. The usual tendency is to get the club head down to the level of the ball by bending the knees, but this is wrong. What you should do is take a stance that is slightly wider than normal—which already lowers you a

When the ball lies well below your feet, you should address the shot with a wide stance.

little—then keep your knees straight and bend your back until the club head can address the ball. Your knees should not bend but, on the other hand, they should not be rigidly stiff. Take the club straight back when you start the backswing and concentrate on bringing it straight down through the ball. Naturally, there will be certain restrictions throughout the swing, so you should hit a seven iron, for example, when you want to get nine-iron distance. Do not worry about having to take a half or three-quarter swing at the ball. This is actually a help, for it reduces the normal tendency of this shot to hook or slice, depending on the lie.

With the knees flexed but not bent, you choke down on the club and lean well over the ball.

Two to try when

coming through the rye

It may not happen often, but every now and then the weekend golfer hits a shot so far off line that it strays into an area of his golf course that was never really intended for play—a place where the rough is knee-deep. Usually he takes an unplayable lie, or hacks it out in three or four shots and tries to forget the whole thing. The pros, on the other hand, rarely face such a shot. But at the 1966 British Open in Muirfield, we all received a reminder of what high rough is like. The grass bordering the fairways at Muirfield not only was a foot to 18 inches deep, it was topped with a heavy head of grain that caused the stalks to droop.

Two types of shots are involved when the rough is this deep: one for when you are a considerable distance from the green, the other for when you are just at the edge of it. On the longer shot you must

surrender any hope of trying to reach the green. Your goal is merely to get the ball onto the side of the fairway that will best open up the green for the next shot. By doing this, you may reduce what seems to be a certain loss of one stroke to something like half a stroke. You should use a wedge or a nine iron, because these clubs have enough loft to get the ball up quickly and enough clubhead weight to fight through the grass. The blade should be opened at address, for the grass will grip the clubhead as it comes down and tend to close the face. The backswing should be upright to reduce the quantity of grass

that must be mowed through, and the downswing hard, with the left hand extremely firm. You won't get much distance, but you should be able to hit far enough to reach the proper side of the fairway.

An explosion shot is the best answer to deep grass around the greens, though it takes a little nerve. You should hit two or three inches behind the ball, just as if hitting from sand, and emphasize the follow-through, for that is what gets the ball up. The explosion shot out of deep grass behaves the same way it would if hit from sand, landing softly and not rolling very far.

It matters if you wiggle a toe

One excuse that you do not hear for a poor golf shot is: "I didn't use enough right foot that time." Well, it may surprise you, but the neglected right foot could very well rate at the top of the excuse list— along with such old favorites as "I didn't keep my head down" and "I tried to kill the ball." The reason is that minor changes in the position of the right foot at address can have a significant effect on the trajectory of a golf shot. When you want to hit a normal shot you should have the toe of your right foot either square to the line of flight or turned out to the right just a bit. This helps you take the club head away from the ball low, make a good turn and start down properly. However, if you need to hit the ball a little higher than normal and perhaps slightly longer, you should point the toe of the right foot farther to the right. This will enable you to make a bigger and stronger turn away from the ball, while still maintaining good balance and rhythm. It also helps keep your hips behind the ball at impact and brings the club head into the ball with more of a sweeping motion, thus getting the ball into the air higher and faster. But if you want a low shot—say you are hitting into the wind or must avoid some low-hanging branches—try turning your right foot slightly to the left. This will restrict your backswing and set up more of a punching action on the downswing, thus keeping the shot low.

Dark red arrow shows foot position that will add height to a shot. Center arrow is the normal position. A further shift (light arrow) will result in a low shot.

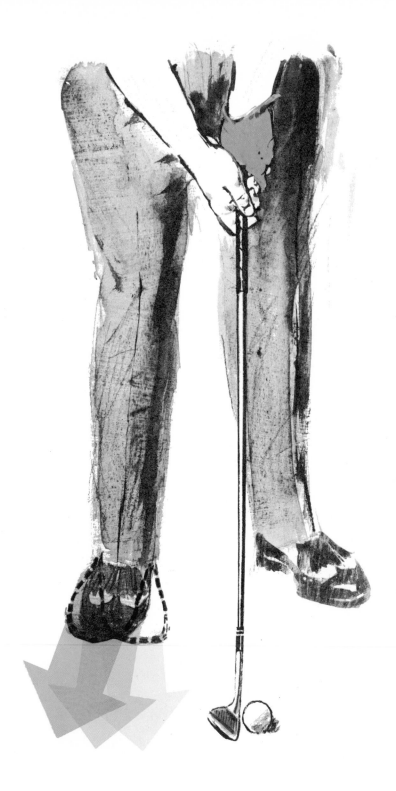

The club should not be swung back any farther than this vertical position. Weight is on the left foot.

The downswing brings the club head into the ball quite sharply and along a slightly outside-in arc.

Try using half a swing
for the half-pitch shot

The 50-yard pitch shot is a consternation causer for the weekend golfer. At address he wonders, "Should I take a long, free backswing and float the ball up there?" He decides to, and about halfway back he thinks, "I should have choked down on the grip, taken a short backswing and punched the ball." This unhappy confusion is unnecessary, for the 50-yard wedge shot, which is really a half-pitch, is easy enough to execute. It is assumed, of course, that the terrain between your ball and the green includes some obstruction—a bunker, water or a hill— so it is imperative that you get the ball well up into the air and drop it onto the green. To start, take your regular stance and grip, but open the club face slightly. Remember that in order to put enough backspin on the ball you will have to strike it quite crisply. Your weight is on your left side. Now start the club up and back rather abruptly, but don't jerk it away. Think of trying to lift it almost straight up in a smooth motion, and just a little to the outside of the line of flight. The backswing should be short because you are hitting the ball only about 50 yards. When you come down into the ball, hit through it very sharply with the left hand as well as the right. The swing should have a firm feel. Even though the backswing has been restricted, this is in no sense a punch shot, so do not think of it as one.

Standing firm in the pines

Most golfers become uneasy when they are confronted with a shot from pine needles. They usually attempt to pick the ball off cleanly, and frequently this results in hitting the ball too thin and not getting it up into the air. This approach to the shot is wrong. Instead of trying to pick the ball off the pine needles, pretend that it is sitting on fairway grass. The swing should be exactly the same as for a fairway shot. You can even hook or fade the ball off pine needles if the occasion demands, and a chip shot off them will have backspin just as a normal chip would. There are two things to remember: (1) take an especially firm stance, making sure that your spikes are set into the ground to prevent slipping, and (2) do not ground the club head behind the ball because there is a good chance the ball will move which will cost you a two-stroke penalty.

When on pine needles the stance should be taken cautiously and club head must not be grounded.

When a golfer starts hitting the ground behind the ball instead of the ball itself, he is doing what is called "hitting fat." It is an infuriating habit to fall into, easy on the ball but awfully hard on the score and the ego. Fortunately, it is an ailment that can be cured easily. The problem is usually nothing more than a head that is changing its plane during the swing and thus changing the plane of the swing itself. This happens in two different ways. You may be dipping your head just before impact, thus lowering the level of the swing. Younger golfers are prone to do this. Or you may be allowing your head to sway to

When the head sways back from its initial position (red disk) the golfer will very likely hit behind the ball.

Go have your head examined

the right during the backswing. This shifts the plane of the swing to the right. The cure, obviously, is to keep a steady head throughout the swing. If hitting fat is a mistake you frequently make, try some practice shots while a friend watches to see if your head is dipping or swaying. If it is dipping, just stop it, primarily by concentrating on holding firm. If it is swaying, you can help yourself by pushing down hard against the inside of the right foot during the backswing, thus thwarting any tendency to shift the head to the right.

When the head dips below its proper position the plane of the swing shifts, causing club to hit in back of the ball.

You can learn

from a telltale divot mark

The golf swing takes place so rapidly that it is often impossible to detect the key mistake that causes a bad shot. There is one way, however, to find some important clues. You can compare the direction of the divot mark with the trajectory of the shot.

The most obvious example of what I mean is supplied by the divot mark that cuts across the line to the target from right to left. This significant mark in the turf has obviously been created by an outside-in swing. If the club face was closed at impact the shot will be pulled to the left. If the club face was square, the shot will slice.

But more subtle clues to faults in the swing can also be found in divots. If the divot mark goes straight toward the target but the ball goes to the left, it has probably been hit with a closed club face. This is usually the result when too much right hand has been applied to the shot just before impact. If the divot mark is straight but the ball starts to the right and slices even farther right, the ball has been hit with an open club face. This is often caused by the hands getting too far ahead of the ball at impact. If the divot mark starts straight and then veers left, you have probably shifted too much weight on to the left foot and let the left side give way—or collapse.

A divot mark pointing left of the hole means the club head came outside in, a mistake that is otherwise hard to detect because the shot may go either left or right.

A woodsman's chop

cuts through an impossible lie

A couple of years ago during the British Open, Phil Rodgers taught me a unique sand shot, one that I did not have to use, I hasten to add, when I beat Phil for the championship in the final round. The situation occurs when the ball is in the sand very near the back bank of the bunker, and the bunker wall is so steep that you cannot draw the club back in the normal fashion.

I tried this shot a hundred different ways before Rodgers solved it for me. There is no problem setting your feet, so assume your normal trap-shot stance. Now just pick the club straight up, breaking your arms just as you would if you were picking up an ax to chop a piece of wood. Then hit down about two inches behind the ball with some extremely strong right-hand action. There cannot be any follow-through at all, because the club head must bury itself in the sand. The arc of the shot is up and down, not back and forth. You may look like a woodcutter, but the result is gratifying.

The club is lifted straight up, with the left elbow bending sharply, and then slammed deep into sand behind ball.

An open approach

for a treacherous sand

Frequently on the pro tour we encounter bunkers filled with a type of sand that is unusually white, quite pretty and very difficult to play out of. This sand, which is known as glass sand, is used at many good courses. Unfortunately, it is so soft and fine that, instead of resisting the force of the club head and thus bounding it up toward the ball, it tends to pull the club head down, which prevents the explosion effect that you get with a normal bunker shot. As a result, you need a different shot for glass sand. First, open the face of the wedge to allow the club's rounded flange to create more of a bounce effect than it usually would. This will counteract the tendency of the sand to force the club head down too deep. Take the club back on a fairly low trajectory, resisting the natural impulse to pick it up too sharply, and come into the ball from only a slight outside-in angle instead of the decidedly outside-in swing used in the normal explosion shot. The club head will not take a lot of sand, and so you won't get much backspin on the shot, but the ball will get up and out of the bunker.

The shot from glass sand requires an open club face and a backswing that is low (green arrow) rather than abrupt (red).

In a situation as bad as the one shown here, the object is not so much to find a shot that will work as it is to find a shot that has *any* chance of working. The ball is on hardpan, the trap is shallow but has a lip, and the green is very narrow. Should you hit your wedge, realizing that it will be difficult, if not impossible, to put enough spin on the ball for it to hold the green? Or should you take a two iron, roll the ball through the sand and hope by some miracle it won't catch the lip of the trap? These might seem to be the only alternatives, and neither of

When the green is too narrow to hold a pitch and the edge of the trap too high to run the ball through, unusual methods are called for.

them has much chance of succeeding. But there is a third shot, one that demands neither an impossible degree of skill nor unbelievable luck. You can try to skip the ball through the trap on one bounce, like a rock skipping off water. Use either a five or a six iron, and hood the faces lightly to get hook overspin on the ball. Chip the ball firmly toward a level place in the sand near the front of the bunker. You will be surprised how frequently the ball hits the sand and pops up onto the green.

A small chip can beat a big blast

When you walk into a bunker carrying anything but a sand wedge your opponents are likely to give you that subtle half sneer which implies you are (1) a hacker and (2) gutless. Well, lots of times you should give them a sneer right back, for there are numerous occasions when the chip shot is by far the best way to get a ball out of sand and close to the hole. Two things must be checked first: The trap should have little or no lip, because the chip is going to take off low and never climb much, and there should be considerable putting surface

Ball is played off right foot, and club face (narrow line) is closed with respect to target line (red arrow).

between the trap and the cup. Assuming these conditions are met, you can hand the sand wedge back to the caddie—caddies disapprove of this shot, too—and ask for an eight or nine iron. Play the ball back toward the right foot, to insure that you will hit down firmly on the ball. You must not hit the sand behind the ball. Choke the club down a couple of inches, and hood the face slightly. Now concentrate hard, keeping the head especially steady, because the shot is a delicate one. The ball will come out crisply, and with considerable overspin, so you can expect a good deal of run. One way to judge how firmly to hit it is to consider how hard you would swing at the same chip shot if the ball were on grass, then hit this one a little easier.

The ball must be hit firmly, and on the downswing, with no sand being moved until after contact with ball.

How you can survive an explosion

The two most important things to keep in mind when exploding from sand are (1) that the swing should be a normal one and (2) that the grip should be choked down somewhat at address. Too many people climb into a sand trap already paralyzed by fear and suddenly start doing things with their swing that they would never think of doing on the fairway. They stab or they dip or they lurch, and they leave the ball in the sand more often than they get it out. The explosion is much the same as any other shot, only your aiming point changes since you are trying to hit a spot in the sand some one to three inches behind the ball instead of the ball itself. Begin by picking the spot—perhaps marked by a discolored grain of sand—and concentrate as hard on hitting it as you would on hitting the ball. The shot should be played pretty much like a short pitch, with the ball off the left heel and the stance slightly open. At address you will have dug your feet into the sand one or two inches to insure a firm stance. This means the ball is that much nearer your hands than usual. You must compensate for this by choking down on the grip. How far you choke down determines how far the ball will fly. This is because distance is controlled more by how deeply underneath the ball the club head digs than by how hard you swing or by how far behind the ball you hit. For a long blast, therefore, you should choke down farther.

Play sand shot with an open stance (arrow shows target line), feet dug in and club choked down to compensate for lower plane of the feet.

You don't need sand

to use a sand wedge

You can find more uses for your sand wedge outside of a bunker than in it. In fact, I use mine for pitching more often than I do my pitching wedge. It has approximately three degrees more loft than the standard pitching wedge and a considerably heavier, more rounded flange. This makes it especially valuable for those delicate short shots that must fly over a trap or mound and then stop on the green, for the sand wedge gets the ball up quickly and with backspin. I also almost always use my sand wedge for pitch shots within 65 yards of the green, even when I am in the center of the fairway and there is no intervening trouble. I do this because the greater loft allows me to go ahead and hit the ball fairly hard. You are less likely to miss a shot when you do not have to baby it. The sand wedge also has many other uses. Try it from the rough, where the heavy blade and flange get under the ball more effectively than a pitching wedge, or from loose or sandy turf, where you need to play an explosion or cut shot. The pitching wedge would probably dig into the turf, but the rounded flange of the sand wedge will bounce up.

When there are no such special advantages to be gained by using the sand wedge and you are in doubt whether to use it or the pitching wedge, then I recommend that you try the pitching wedge. The fact that the pitching wedge has less weight and loft, while a disadvantage in the situations mentioned above, makes it a little easier to control.

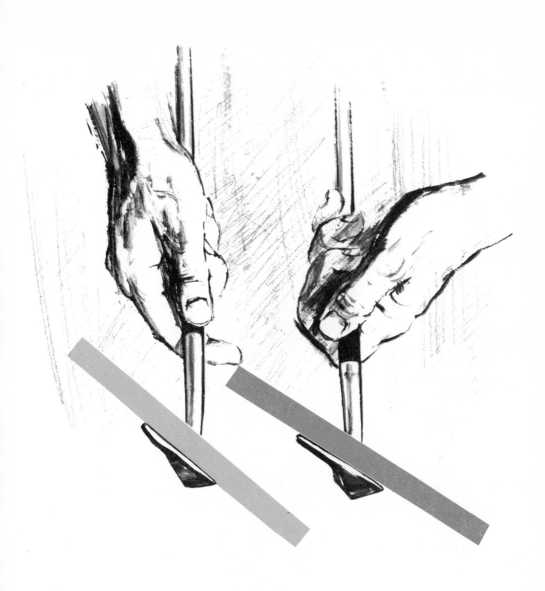

Because the sand wedge (right) has more loft and flange than the pitching wedge (left) it is the best club for many special shots.

A neglected shot

to keep you out of trouble

Too many weekend golfers think they should try to hit their short approaches close to the hole on the fly with a pitching wedge when they would be far better advised to play one of the game's oldest and soundest shots—the pitch-and-run. It is not hard to learn, and once mastered it can, given the proper conditions, be an extraordinarily useful and satisfying shot. The proper conditions are encountered very often: windy days, hard greens and/or a flat golf course.

The main reason for not shooting right at the flagstick with the wedge is that, while the results can often be spectacular, they are often spectacularly dismal. It is simply a very difficult shot to execute successfully. The pitch-and-run, on the other hand, can be equally successful at its best, and is rarely a disaster at its worst.

The basic thing to keep in mind about the pitch-and-run, of course, is that the ball is going to roll a long distance. It must be played to land on flat ground. It can be hit with a wedge—by closing the face and playing the ball well back toward the right foot—but best results are usually achieved with a seven or eight iron. Play the ball at about the middle of the stance and choke down on the grip two inches or so, as shown at left. Take an upright, short backswing and concentrate on meeting the ball firmly. The club should hit the ball before hitting the grass, or the necessary crispness and control will be lost. Until you have practiced the shot enough to see how it behaves, it is probably wise to hit it harder than you think necessary. You are not likely to be penalized severely if the ball does go past the hole.

Be sure the club meets the ball before the grass.

Make your putter suit your game

It is generally agreed that a heavy putter is more effective on slow greens, such as the Bermuda grass of the South, and that a light one is better on the fast bent-grass greens often encountered in the North. Unfortunately, this theory has led a great many golfers who play a variety of courses to conclude that they should carry both a light and a heavy putter and switch according to the speed of the greens. This is something I advise against. It is difficult enough to adjust to an unfamiliar putting surface without also having to adjust to a change in putters as well. When I first joined the pro tour I used the light blade putter that I had found so effective on the bent-grass greens of the kind of courses that most major amateur tournaments are played on. But it was out of my bag for good after five weeks because it seemed that no two courses on the pro tour had putting surfaces of the same speed. I made a successful switch to a blade putter that is built up to medium weight by having a thick flange on the back of the head, and that is the only putter I use. By all means use a light putter if you play only fast greens and a heavy-headed one if you consistently play on slow greens. But if you are a golfer who travels a lot and you like to play on many different types of courses, I suggest you find yourself a medium-weight putter and stick with it.

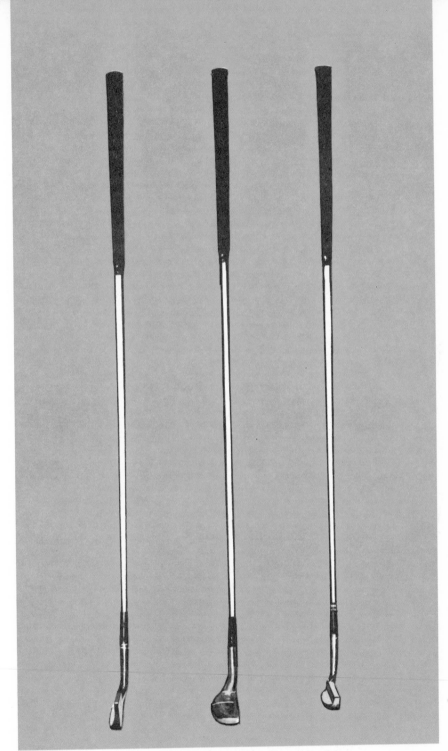

A blade putter (left) is best for fast greens, while a heavy putter is best for slow greens. The putter that I use (right) is a combination of the two styles.

Startling as the thought may be, practice does not make you a good putter. What I mean is that you cannot become a good putter by going out on the practice green every day and hitting a hundred balls at the hole. Putting is strictly a matter of feel, touch and timing, and these are the only things you should work for on the putting green. When I practice my putting, I want to get to the point where I know what I am doing throughout my putting stroke. I want to make sure there is a fluid feeling between my hands and the actual putting stroke. I practice only until I achieve a constant rhythm, with the blade hitting the ball firmly and the ball coming squarely off the putter head. When I feel this rhythm six or seven times in a row, I quit. If you work at your putting past that point you will become mechanized and lose your sense of touch. So practice until you feel you are putting well, and then stop before you spoil your stroke.

The putting stroke is a matter of feel between the firmness in the hands and the firmness with which the putter strikes the ball.

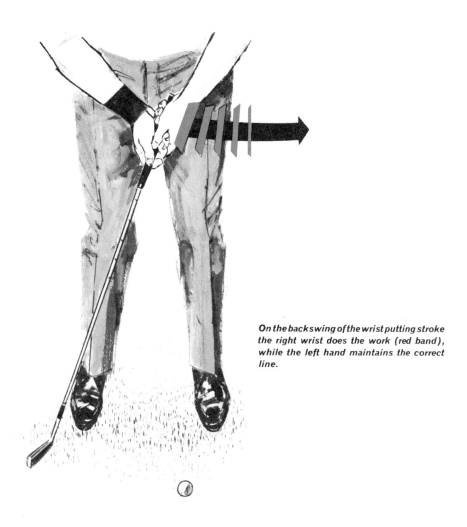

On the backswing of the wrist putting stroke the right wrist does the work (red band), while the left hand maintains the correct line.

Know what your hands are up to

There are two schools of thought on putting. One calls for you to break your wrists. The other requires you to keep your wrists firm and move the arms instead. But regardless of which you follow, you should know the role that each hand plays in the putting stroke. Like most touring pros, I am a wrist putter. The back of my left hand points toward the hole at address. I let my right hand do the work of taking the club back. My left hand is essentially acting only as a guide. The hands work the same way on the forward stroke, the right hand doing the hitting and the left hand keeping the club head on line. If the left hand were to stop guiding at impact, the ball would veer right or left. An arm putter—and until fairly recently I was one—must use his hands differently. In this style the left hand does more of the work. As before, it does all of the guiding, but it also takes the putter back. The right hand is emphasized only during the striking of the ball. It really makes little difference whether you become a wrist putter or an arm putter. But try to master one or the other and stick with it. Do not switch back and forth from round to round.

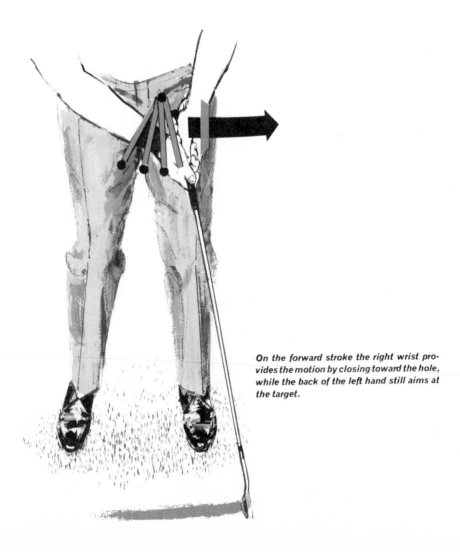

On the forward stroke the right wrist provides the motion by closing toward the hole, while the back of the left hand still aims at the target.

Distance can best be judged by mentally marking it off in five- or ten-foot intervals.

Where headwork

means more than the swing

Every golf shot combines two basic elements. One is judging distance and the effect of wind or terrain on the ball. The other is the execution of the swing. In putting, the mental calculations are more important than in any other shot—and more difficult—but there are ways to help yourself. Many golfers simply pace the distance to the cup. I don't recommend that. Instead, stand over the ball and look at the line to the hole, simultaneously measuring the distance in five- or ten-foot intervals. Then check the texture of the grass and remember these few tips: you obviously do not have to hit a putt as hard when the grass grows toward the cup as when it grows toward you, but the grain can be difficult to see. In Florida grass grows toward the setting sun; in California it grows toward the ocean. With both bent and Bermuda grass the grain is with you when the grass looks slick and shiny, and it is against you when it looks dull and dark.

An overspin stroke

smooths a bumpy route

One important factor when putting on spiked or bumpy greens is the necessity for controlling the ball at, and immediately after, impact. A putt that is stroked in the normal way has almost no spin as it leaves the club head. For the first few inches—depending on the length of the putt—the ball is essentially skidding. Then it begins to pick up its

own rotation and rolls toward the hole. When greens are unusually bumpy, this lack of initial spin becomes a problem, because the ball may well hit something quite small and be deflected before it develops its own inertia. Any fraction of an inch that the ball is knocked off line early, of course, becomes a couple of feet by the time it reaches the hole. To help solve the control problem with such a putt, I suggest that you try hitting it on the upswing. This slight change in the stroke will give the ball overspin from the moment it leaves the club head. The overspin will help the ball remain on line through those important first few inches.

Instead of using a normal putting stroke that makes the ball skid (left), you should hit the ball slightly high (right) to give it overspin.

An awful putt

showed me how to win

At the 1966 Masters, the fairways were hard and so were the greens. Because of this the tournament committee decided it would be best not to mow the greens and the fairways too closely, for fear the dry wind that was blowing across the course each day might kill what grass was left. Many players felt the pin placements were as demanding as they had ever been. Possibly this was a factor too, but I think the condition of the course was really what made the scores so high.

In addition to the difficult conditions, I was having problems with my own game that made scoring tough. After the first round my putting stroke completely deserted me, and I had serious problems with my concentration that stayed with me until the last nine holes of the playoff.

The putting problem I solved—in the world's luckiest way. On Sunday afternoon more millions of people than I care to think about

This drawing is based on the video tape I saw of my missed putt on 17. I noticed my head was too far forward, causing me to line up to the left (solid line) instead of toward the right corner of cup (dotted line).

watched me blow a three-footer on the 17th hole that could have won the tournament and retrieved all of my earlier mistakes. I had aimed the putt just inside the right-hand corner of the hole, but when I hit it the ball broke so far to the left, even though I stroked it firmly, that it never came close. To be frank, I looked like a duffer choking up with a $1 Nassau at stake. But I knew nerves had nothing to do with it. For some reason I had hit the putt miserably.

A little while later I was watching as CBS did a video-tape replay of the putt on television, and I spotted what was wrong. On Thursday I had putted well. On Friday I needed 38 putts, and I missed seven of them from five feet or less. On Saturday and Sunday my putting was almost as bad as Friday's. What I saw in the TV picture was that I was lined up incorrectly. My head was bent too far forward, so I was actually looking back at the ball and the blade of the putter (*page 114*). I thought I was squaring the blade to the line along which I wanted to stroke the ball, but this was only an illusion. In reality I was lined up too far to the left. I went to the putting green Sunday night and practiced with my head in the correct position. During Monday's playoff I did not hit a single bad putt.

"What's wrong with Nicklaus?"

I guess there are times in the life of any athlete when circumstances force him to ask himself, "Am I really any good?" Never mind all his old press clippings; forget the self-confidence that he has had to build within himself to have any chance of success. Just face up to that simple question. It is a question that I had to ask myself after I failed to make the cut at the 1967 Masters, and a lot of other people were asking it, too. "What's wrong with Nicklaus? Has he lost it already?"

Suddenly I began to wonder if perhaps I had played badly the last five years. Maybe I had been lucky to win my six major championships. So I put it to myself: "What *is* wrong with Jack Nicklaus?" And that was when I began to win the U.S. Open at Baltusrol, a victory that has to rank as the most gratifying of my career.

In a way this Open had everything for me. I made changes in my swing, and they worked. Two days before play began I made a major shift in my putting stroke, and rarely have I putted better. Just when I was looking for a new putter somebody handed me one. The course turned out to be superb. I was paired for two days with the man I like most to play golf against—my friend Arnold Palmer—and was able to beat him. And, of course, I broke the Open scoring record.

There is no question that I had been playing bad golf prior to the Open. I was hooking my drives, hitting my iron shots—especially the short ones—quite indifferently and putting worse than I can ever remember. At the Masters, all three of these things caught up with me at once, and it was no surprise that I missed the cut. I deserved to.

It was then that I did my thinking and made my initial decision. Once I had been a fine golfer, hitting the ball left to right, but I had

turned away from that style of play. Now I had to give up hooking the ball and go back to my old swing. It was this that I worked on through April and May, and the results showed at Baltusrol. Throughout the entire tournament I did not hit one hook, I did not have one shot move from right to left.

In addition, I made two other technical adjustments. One concerned my short game, which had been so erratic. I have to keep my left arm rigid on such shots, and soon after the Masters I realized that I was not doing this. I was letting it flop around in the breeze. As a result, the club head was on a different trajectory every time I came into the ball. I never knew where the shot was going. To correct this, I began to concentrate on my left arm as I swung, and I started doing stretching exercises every day—the same kind you do if you have bursitis—that would make it easier for me to keep the arm rigid. This

Here is the change—shown for a 12-footer—that I made in my putting. Instead of taking the club far back (left), I made the stroke very short (right).

paid off with approach shots in the Open that seemed to me to be constantly on the flag.

When you hit the ball at the pin you obviously take the pressure off your putting. You don't have to go through the worry of trying to get down in two from 40 and 50 feet on every green. But when I arrived at Baltusrol for some practice a week before the tournament, I was still putting poorly. I brought about half a dozen putters with me, none of which I really liked.

One evening I was standing on the putting green with Deane Beman and I borrowed his putter. It felt super to me. Pretty soon Deane had his hand out, wanting it back. He saw the look in my eye, and wasn't about to give that putter away. But he said he had a few more in the car similar to it, and a friend of his, Fred Mueller, an amateur golfer from Washington, went to get them. Mueller also

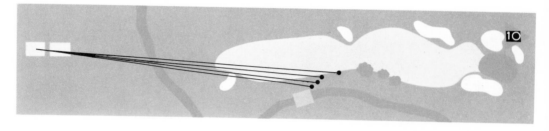

This is where I hit my four tee shots on the hole that gave me the most trouble, the 449-yard tenth, on which I went three over par.

brought back his own putter, the head of which he had dipped in white paint. It sure looked strange. I didn't care for Deane's rejects—they felt different from the one he was using—but that white one was perfect. I borrowed it from Fred and practiced with it back in Columbus all that weekend.

Now I was more confident about my putting, but it was not until Tuesday night at Baltusrol that the really important thing happened. Gordon Jones, a friend of mine on the tour, was watching me stroke the ball. I was trying some different things, obviously displeased, and he said, "Jack, why don't you go back to the way you used to putt years ago. You know, take it back a little shorter and then hit it harder." Well, it was like a bell had started ringing. Unconsciously, over a period of time, I had let my putting stroke get longer and longer. This meant I was actually slowing the club head down as it approached the ball. You can't do that with any golf shot. And right there, with Jones watching, I began to take a very short backswing and rap in putts from everywhere. The next day it seemed I sank them all, and I shot my practice-round 62. I couldn't miss with that White Fang, and I continued to putt well throughout the tournament, three-putting only three greens while one-putting seventeen. Of the five key shots I hit, four were putts.

This week I ordered half a dozen of those putters. I'll send one to Fred, of course, but I hope he will let me keep the one he loaned me. Deane is right. Lending a putter is dangerous.

Don't let your golf be a dirty business

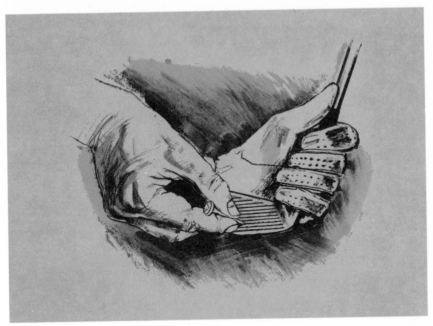

To insure maximum backspin, use a tee and clean out the grooves of the club face before hitting an iron.

Too many weekend golfers ignore what seems to them to be a trivial part of the game, care of their clubs. As often as not they keep their clubs at home, and they find it quite easy not to clean them. But this costs strokes. If the grooves of an iron are not clean, the club head will not put maximum backspin on the ball. During a round you should have a towel available so that the club face can be wiped clean after every shot. You should also clean the grooves by running a sharp object through them before every shot.

Caring for woods presents a different problem. Woods pick up moisture and are affected by sharp changes from very moist to very dry climates. To prevent any problems, you should soak your woods periodically in linseed oil. This seals the wood and keeps it from absorbing moisture. Some people oil the heads of their irons, presumably to keep them from rusting. I do not do this, and I don't recommend it, because anything that makes the face of the iron slick is likely to affect the flight of the ball.

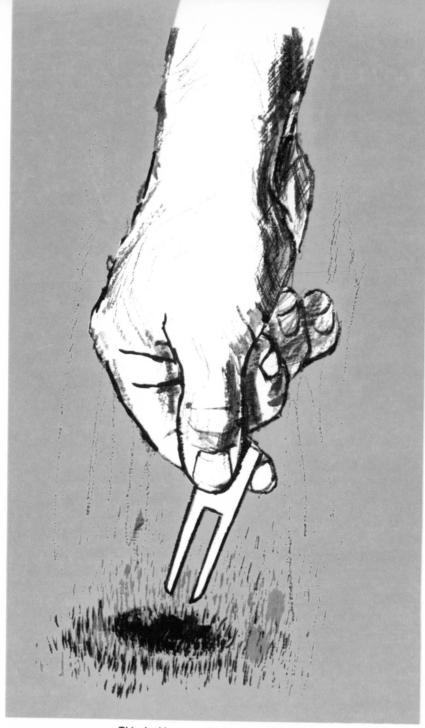

This double-pronged attack on ball marks results in the least possible damage to the putting surface as the turf is carefully raised to its former level.

Save strokes by
being a divot digger

Though greenskeepers may not yearn for the chance to put this idea into action, it could be argued that one way for a golf course to get its greens in shape is to host a professional tournament. The reason is that players on the pro tour, unlike many club members, make a fetish of repairing divot marks on greens—theirs, yours, everybody's. By the divot mark, I mean the indentation made on the green by the biting impact of an approach shot. The pros fix these marks conscientiously because neglecting them scars the green.

Since a carelessly repaired ball mark can affect a putt, I have two kinds of advice for you. First, always examine the line of your putt for ball marks—even old ones—and make the necessary repairs. You might as well not even line up a putt if you are carelessly going to hit it over divots. Second, know how to fix ball marks properly, thus smoothing your path and other people's, too. The best tool I have found for this personal greenskeeping is the new double-pronged aluminum device shown at left. It is very popular on the pro tour and should be generally available soon. The repair work is done from the side of the mark from which the ball was hit. Thrust the prong, or a wooden tee, under the indentation at a fairly sharp angle and lift the mashed dirt area up to green level. There is usually a small flap of turf on the far side of the mark. Lift this flap slightly and pull it back over the bare dirt. Stab the prong into the ground at several points around the outside of the ball mark. Finally, tap the turf carefully with the sole of your putter. If anybody misses a putt over that ball mark now, it isn't your fault.

When a big club suits small boys

There are two ways to outfit a youngster who is just learning to play golf. You can give him dad's old clubs, cut down to fit him, or buy junior-sized clubs. Either method can be effective, depending on the age and size of the child. Two important points must be kept in mind. First, a child should begin with a club that he can manage with ease; otherwise he will have difficulty learning a rhythmic, sound swing. Second, he should start using adult clubs—either cut down or light ones—as soon as he is able to handle them, otherwise the eventual transition may be a difficult one. I advise the following: if the beginner is ten or younger he should definitely use junior clubs. They are light, short and balanced to fit someone who is light and short. These are the clubs with which he should learn the fundamentals. As soon as he shows some proficiency with these, he should start swinging adult clubs cut down to fit his height. This will probably happen at about age eleven or twelve. After he has played for a while with cut-down adult clubs and has grown a little taller, he will find the change to full-length clubs an easy one.

There is a point at which a cut-down adult club (left) is better for children than a specially designed junior club.

It isn't a game of inches

Most tall golfers think they must go through a series of contortions to get themselves into position to hit a golf ball. They do a deep knee bend or they curve their backs or slouch their shoulders, all in an unnecessary effort to get themselves into what they think is the same position that a shorter man appears to manage with such ease. What tall golfers often do not realize is that their hands fall at almost the same position as a shorter man's. I am six feet and I have short arms but, as you can see in the illustration left, my hands are in relatively the same position as the man who is four inches taller. Height is actually an advantage in golf, because a tall person can achieve a symmetrical arc in his swing much more easily than a short person. The tall golfer should forget his height. It is the thinking about it and trying to compensate for it that ruins his swing.

The position of the hands shows why a tall golfer need not compensate for his height.